Molly a Milksnake

Mary Ann Hoffman

NEIGHBORHOOD READERS

Rosen Classroom Books & Materials™

New York

Molly is making a milkshake.

Molly puts in milk.

Molly puts in ice cream.

Molly puts in juice.

Molly puts in strawberries.

Molly puts in bananas.

Molly drinks the milkshake!